1 85103 073 5

First published 1987 by Editions Gallimard
First published 1989 in Great Britain by Moonlight Publishing Ltd,
131 Kensington Church Street, London W8
© 1987 Editions Gallimard
English text © 1989 Moonlight Publishing Ltd

Printed in Italy by La Editoriale Libraria

PIONEERS OF THE AIR

| DISCOVERERS |

Written and illustrated by
James Prunier

Translated by Margaret Malpas

MOONLIGHT PUBLISHING

Contents

Birds	8
Myths and legends	11
A flying man?	12
Imaginary machines	14
Kites	16
Lighter than air	18
Balloons	20
Parachutes	22
Dirigibles	24
Sir George Cayley, the father of air-navigation	28
Heavier than air	30
Clément Ader: powered flight – almost!	32
Otto Lilienthal, the first hang-glider	34
The dawn of the twentieth century	36
Samuel Langley's *Aerodrome*	38
The Wright brothers, master inventors	40
Controlled flight, the first real aeroplanes	42
Santos-Dumont and Ferber	44
The first European flights	46
Propellers and engines	48
The plane-makers	50
The beginning of the aircraft industry	52
Helicopters	54
Crossing the Channel	56
Sea-planes	58
Flights in public	60
Airshows	62
Air-races	64
Long-distance flights	66
On the eve of the First World War	68
An A to Z of aircraft facts	70
Places to visit	75
About the author	76

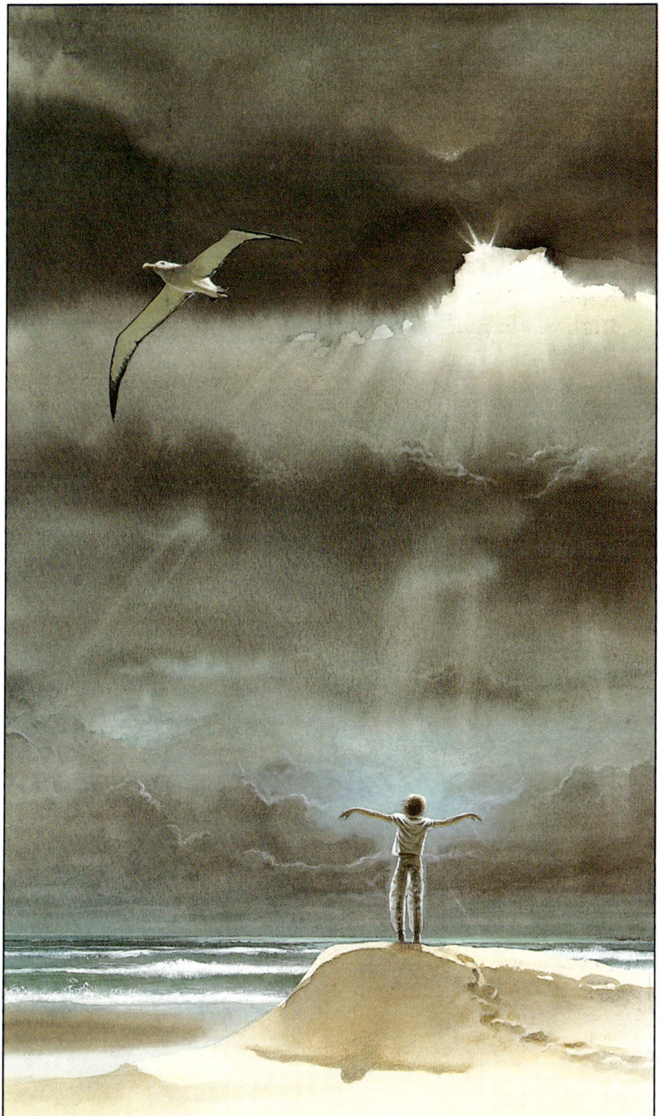

Birds

A pterosaur, a prehistoric flying reptile. Its wings, each supported by a finger, were made of skin.

A fossil archaeopteryx, the oldest known bird

A bird's skeleton is made of bones which are hollow but very strong. Some of these bones are fused together: for instance, the bones of the pelvic girdle, the dorsal and lumbar vertebrae, the collar-bones and shoulder-blades. This makes a strong support for the bird's legs and wings. The breast-bone is a vertical plate to which the pectoral muscles are attached. These very powerful muscles make up 30% of the bird's weight, and control the wing movement.

Archaeopteryx, the ancestor of modern birds, first appeared 150 million years ago. It probably had a very long tail, a jaw with teeth, and scaly legs; so it was descended from reptiles.

But its body was covered with feathers, and its front legs had turned into wings, though these were rudimentary and could probably be used only for gliding.

After the dinosaurs disappeared, 60 million years ago, various kinds of bird gradually developed; today there are 8,600 different species.

A wing: its shape can be adapted for different kinds of flight.

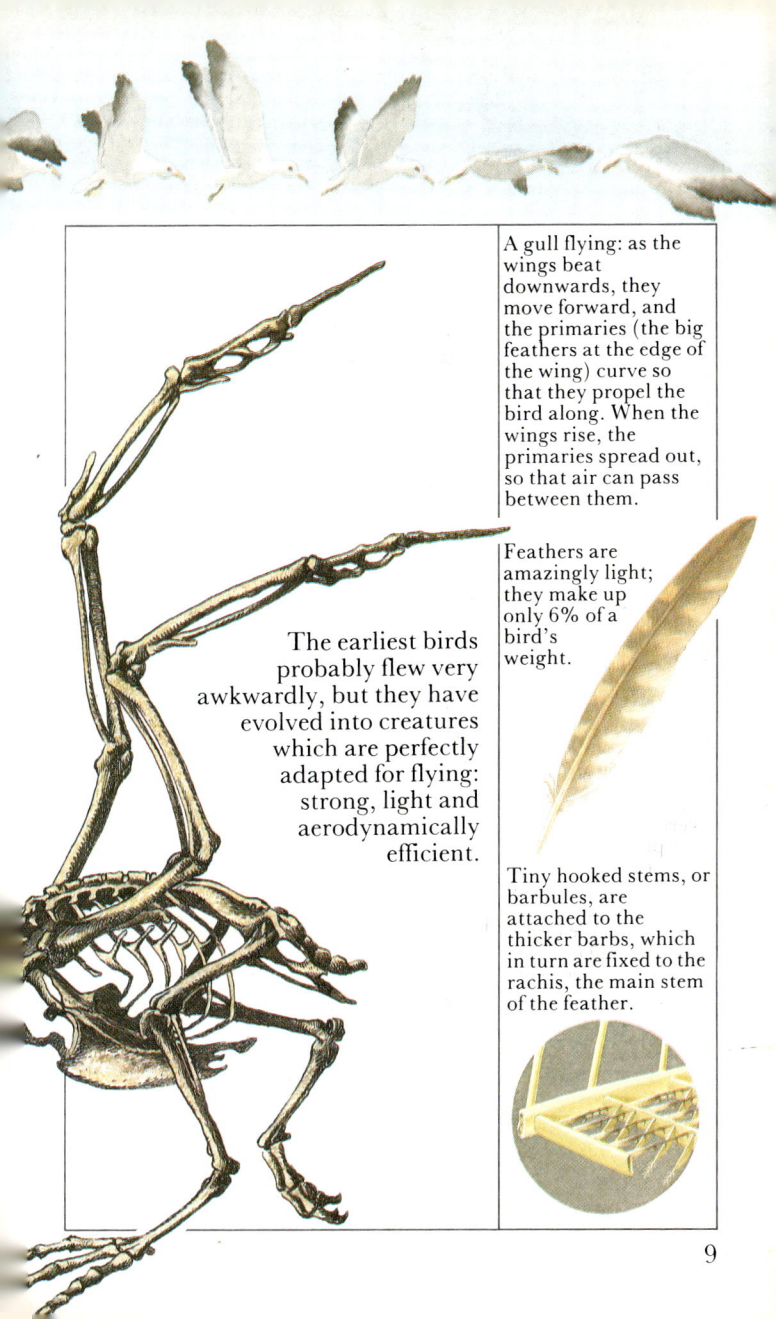

A gull flying: as the wings beat downwards, they move forward, and the primaries (the big feathers at the edge of the wing) curve so that they propel the bird along. When the wings rise, the primaries spread out, so that air can pass between them.

The earliest birds probably flew very awkwardly, but they have evolved into creatures which are perfectly adapted for flying: strong, light and aerodynamically efficient.

Feathers are amazingly light; they make up only 6% of a bird's weight.

Tiny hooked stems, or barbules, are attached to the thicker barbs, which in turn are fixed to the rachis, the main stem of the feather.

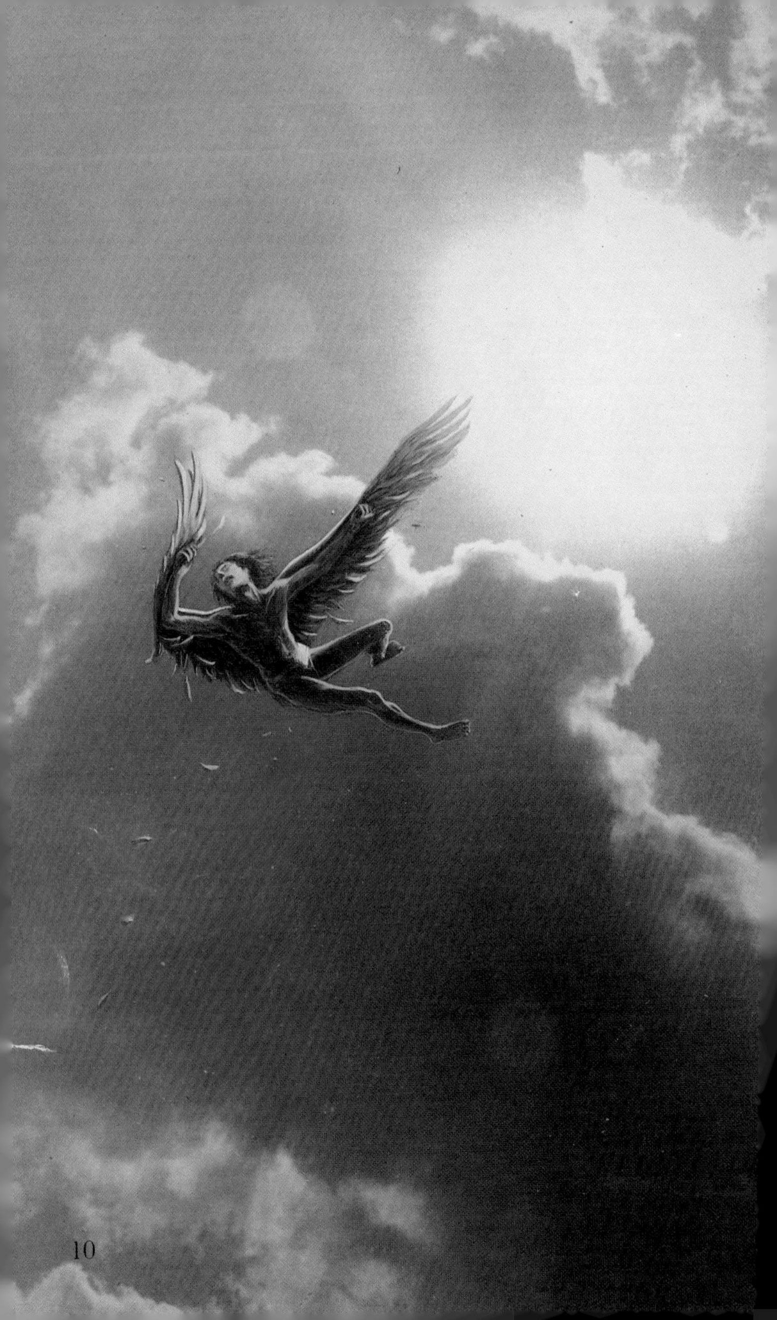

Myths and legends

For thousands of years, people have watched birds flying and tried to imitate them. The myths and legends of early civilisations show their fascination with flight.

In a Greek legend, for instance, Icarus and Daedalus, his father, are imprisoned in King Minos' labyrinth, on Crete. In order to escape, they have to cross the sea, so Daedalus has the idea of making wings out of feathers stuck together with wax.

Fairy-tale magicians from the East fly on magic carpets . . .

Icarus ignores his father's warnings and flies too close to the sun. The wax melts in the heat, and Icarus plummets into the sea.

A Persian legend tells of a king who wanted to rule the sky. First, he has four long poles fixed to his throne, with a leg of mutton tied on top of each. Then four eagles are harnessed to the throne. Desperate to get at the meat, the birds flap their wings violently, and the king is lifted into the air in his strange flying-machine.

In 1680 a French locksmith called Besnier managed to glide from the top of a high tower to the ground, in this 'flapping carriage'.

Could a man learn to fly?

The first men who tried to fly knew nothing about the principles of flight, so the result was always the same: bravely jumping from the tops of high buildings, they crashed to the ground far below. One of them tried to 'fly' from the top of a castle in Scotland, and as he lay on the ground, his leg broken, he insisted that if only he had used eagles' feathers for his wings, instead of hens' feathers, he would quite certainly have been able to fly all the way to France.

Leonardo da Vinci discovered that birds kept their balance in flight by using a special set of feathers, the alula, which he called the 'bastard-wing'.

In the 16th century, Leonardo da Vinci was regarded as the greatest living genius. He studied birds in flight, and worked out how their wings kept them in the air.

From the age of thirty, he spent a lot of time puzzling over the problem of muscular flight, and designed many machines of various degrees of complexity; he produced 500 drawings and 35,000 words on the subject. But his ideas are not practicable. Man simply does not have enough physical strength to fly.

A bird is a machine; it works according to mathematical laws. Man is capable of reproducing all the movements of this machine.
Leonardo da Vinci

Attaching wings to your arms is not the solution...

Leonardo's design for a flying machine with moving wings, which the flyer worked with his hands and feet

13

Imaginary machines

A bat-shaped ornithopter, from an engraving by Heath (1829)

Jules Verne (1828-1905)

Thomas Edison drew this ornithopter in about 1880; it was to be driven by electric motors.

Though men in the 19th century still lacked the technical skill to make flying-machines, they dreamed up the most extraordinary contraptions. Engravings from this period show ornithopters, machines with flapping wings powered by unspecified motors, carrying travellers across continents. On the other hand, some of those working on the problem were still convinced that a man could easily work wings with a lever and thus fly as freely as a bird.

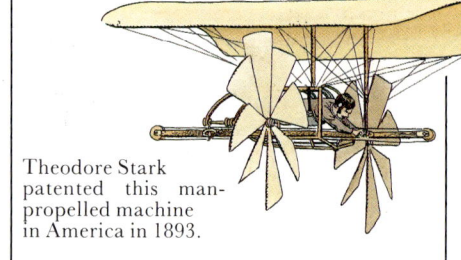

Theodore Stark patented this man-propelled machine in America in 1893.

The French novelist Jules Verne made use of the technical knowledge of his time to dream up the fantastic machines which appear in his adventure stories: for instance, an enormous craft kept in the air by a whole forest of propellers. In one of his stories the flying ship, with propellers at the front and back, sets off on a voyage of discovery, just as the great airborne explorers were to do in real life.

The imaginary flight of the *Ariel*, W S Henson's 'flying steam-coach'

In 1843, William Samuel Henson designed his 'flying steam-coach', which excited everyone involved in aeronautical research. Henson, helped by his colleague John Stringfellow, was the first to devise a **fixed-wing monoplane**, with a tail which functioned as a rudder for both heights and direction, an undercarriage, two propellers (driven by a 25 hp steam-engine), and a fuselage!

Unfortunately there was never enough money to build this forerunner of the modern aircraft: it existed only as a model. Nonetheless, this model 'flew' over the Channel, beyond the Pyramids, even to China, in the form of a picture printed on scarves and handkerchiefs!

William Samuel Henson (1805-1888)

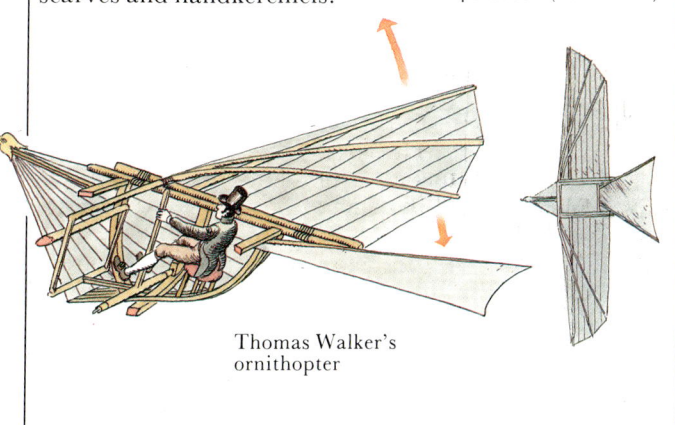

Thomas Walker's ornithopter

15

Kites

Kites from south-east Asia

By the 12th century kites were very common throughout south-east Asia; they were flown at festivals and religious ceremonies, and the Chinese and Japanese even used them to carry spies. Bandits and warriors are said to have ambushed their victims by using kites to travel silently through the air.

One of the earliest European kites, dating from the 14th century

In the 13th century, when Marco Polo's voyages established contact with the East, Europeans discovered kites. They used them as banners, for decoration, or as toys. But Westerners did not find out until the 19th century that the secret of flight lies in the rigid framework of the kite...

George Pocock's 'flying coach'. In 1827 this vehicle, pulled by two specially designed kites, travelled the 65 km between Marlborough and Bristol at a speed of 32 km/h. According to the inventor, it did not jolt or pitch at all.

In 1752 Benjamin Franklin saw lightning strike his kite and run down the string to the earth. This led him to invent the first lightning conductor.

Cellular kite made by Lawrence Hargrave in 1893

In about 1890 an Australian called Laurence Hargrave watched how birds soar and hover, and tried to incorporate the technique in the construction of a kite. He also studied stability and lift, and in 1893 he perfected his cellular kite, made of boxlike structures. The following year, using four of these kites, he managed to rise 5 m off the ground. He had discovered the structural principle of the biplane.

Lighter than air

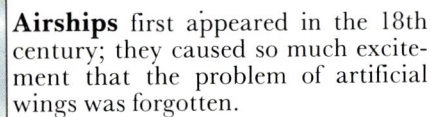

Airships first appeared in the 18th century; they caused so much excitement that the problem of artificial wings was forgotten.

In 1783, Joseph and Etienne Montgolfier, who were paper manufacturers in France, enclosed hot air in a sphere. The idea had occurred to them when they threw a large paper sack on to the fire and watched it rise up the chimney. Other inventors had worked on the same idea, but it was the Montgolfier brothers who succeeded in making the first 'lighter than air' machine, which they displayed publicly on 5 June 1783 at Annonay.

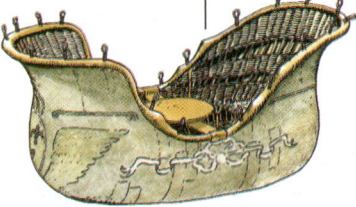

The first balloon flight, in 1783

Slung below the balloon was a basket, or 'nacelle'.

A montgolfière

On 19 September that year, a sheep, a cock and a duck went up in a 'montgolfière': the world's first air-travellers.

On 21 November, the Marquis d'Arlandes and Pilâtre de Rozier became the first men to take to the air when they spent twenty-five minutes aboard a montgolfière. The first woman to fly was Jeanne Labrosse-Garnerin, in 1798.

In 1868, the famous photographer Nadar took the first aerial photographs, and in 1901 the German pilot Berson coaxed his balloon to a height of 10,500 m.

On 7 January 1785 Blanchard and Jeffries succeeded in flying across the Channel.

Even a horse rose into the air, on a specially constructed platform, in 1798.

All sorts of fantastic flying-ships were designed, like the one on the left, drawn by Dunker in 1784.

These feats gradually turned aeronautics into a sport, and balloon trips and races became Sunday treats for the rich.

Balloons in war-time

A balloon was first used for military purposes at the Battle of Fleurus, in 1794. The scout in the balloon sent back his despatches tied to bags of sand, which slid down the hawsers of the balloon. The enemy tried to burst the balloon with their cannon: the first anti-aircraft guns.

The Battle of Fleurus

Balloons

This is how the nacelle is attached to the hoop.

The nacelle (8) is a wicker basket which hangs from the hoop (6). The weight of the nacelle is spread evenly over the whole surface of the canopy by means of a net made of hemp (3). The canopy itself (4) is made of a light, closely-woven material, strengthened and made waterproof by a coating of varnish or rubber. It is inflated through a narrow mouth (5).

How a gas balloon works

Balloons rise because the gas inside them is less dense than the surrounding air. To fly higher still, the pilot unloads bags of sand, one by one (9), and to drop down he pulls a cord to open a valve (2), which releases some gas. When the balloon is near the ground, the trail rope (7) is thrown down to show the pilot how far above the ground he is. On landing, the rip panel (1) has to be opened, so that the gas can escape quickly; otherwise the wind would drag the inflated balloon along the ground.

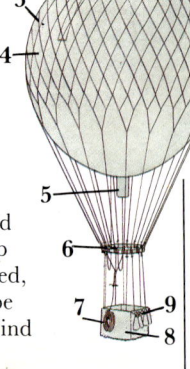

In 1870 Gambetta, the French Minister of the Interior, escaped from the Siege of Paris by balloon.

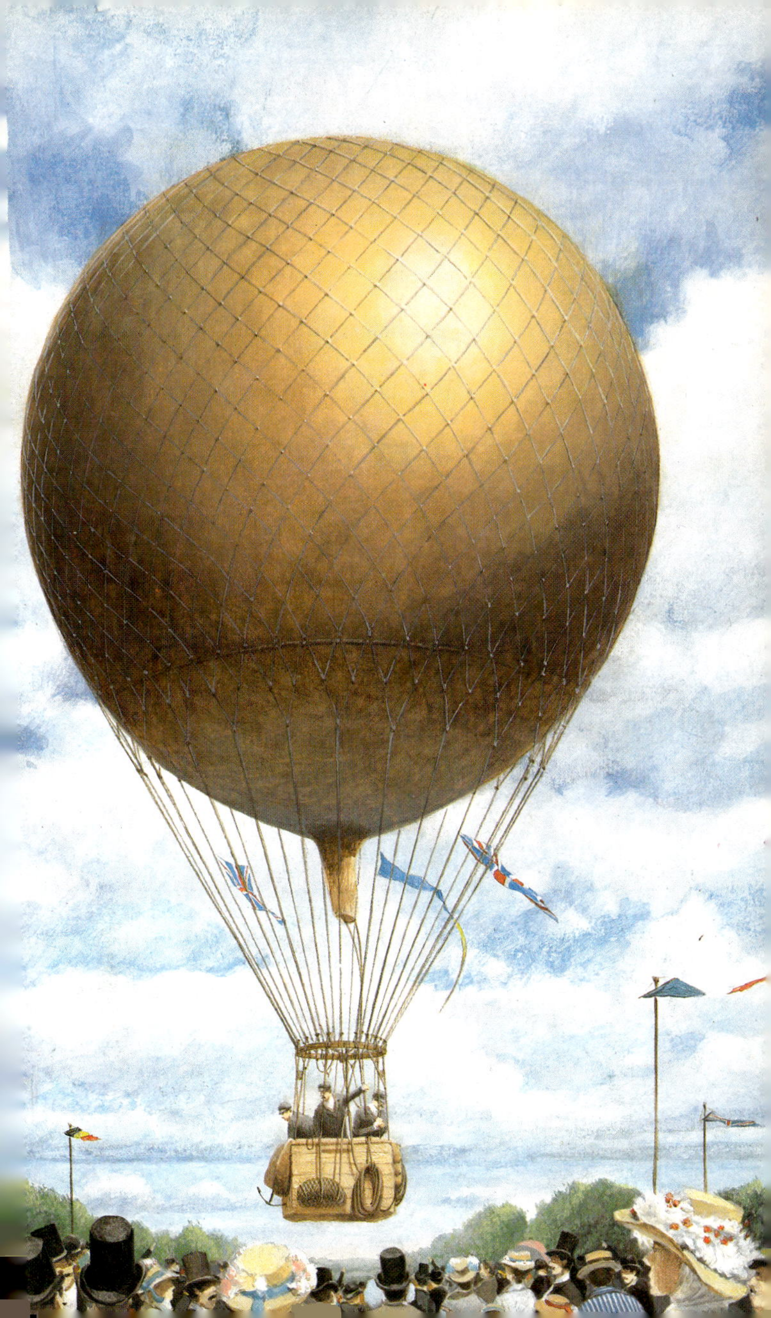

Parachutes

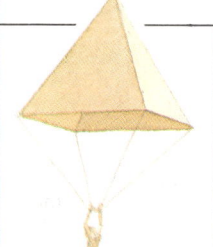

At Cordoba in 852, when people were still trying to fly from the tops of towers, an Arab scholar called Firman is said to have floated to earth as air was trapped in the folds of his cloak – the very first parachute.

Two centuries before the first parachute jump Leonardo designed this kite-like device, which incorporates most of the basic principles of the parachute.

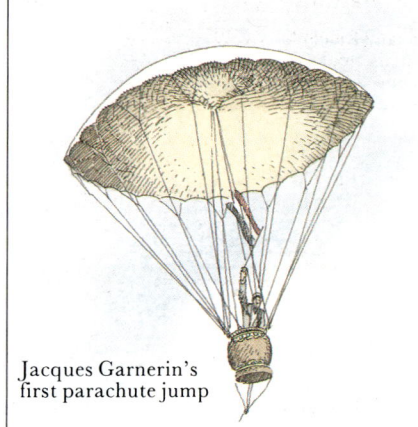

Jacques Garnerin's first parachute jump

A parachute basket belonging to Mme Poitevin, a French woman who made 571 'flights', using the technique devised by Elisa Garnerin.

The first person to work out the **principle of the parachute** was Leonardo da Vinci: 'Why shouldn't one use the air to act as a brake as one descends?' His scheme was not quite right, but the essential idea is there.

In 1784, Lenormand, Blanchard and the Montgolfier brothers carried out some experiments, but it was Jacques Garnerin who tested his design on animals and then had the courage to jump out of a balloon himself, on 22 October 1797, and float to earth beneath his parachute. Admittedly, his device was not stable and his landing was uncontrolled; he should have made an opening at the top of the dome of the parachute, to allow the air to escape smoothly. This was what was missing from Leonardo's design too.

In 1837 Robert Cocking, a 61-year-old painter, tried to improve the parachute by inverting its shape. The basket plummeted to the ground, and Cocking was killed.

Franz Reichelt in his cloak-cum-parachute.

Women too were bold pioneers. Garnerin's wife, Jeanne Labrosse-Garnerin, the first woman to go up in a balloon, was also the first woman parachutist. Most famous of all was Garnerin's niece Elisa, who drew the crowds by carrying out forty parachute jumps between 1815 and 1836.

On 4 February 1912, the Austrian tailor Franz Reichelt, wearing a sort of parachute-cloak, tried to glide down from the first floor of the Eiffel Tower. As he leapt he called out, 'See you soon!' Five seconds later, he crashed to the ground.

Dirigibles

Balloons are unfortunately at the mercy of the wind. To get round this problem, people decided to build an airship which could be propelled and steered, a 'dirigible'.

To glide through the air, a dirigible has to have an **aerodynamic shape**: an elongated canopy. To maintain this shape the gas pressure has to be very high, or the flexible canopy will collapse. As the balloon rises, however,

Henri Giffard's dirigible (1852) was the first to fly, at 10 km/h, but was only partially controllable.

the pressure increases still further and the crew have to release some of the gas to prevent the balloon exploding. But this means that when the balloon comes down again, the canopy is slack and inefficient because the gas pressure is reduced, and so the crew must then inflate the small bags of air inside the canopy, until it returns to its proper shape.

Larger dirigibles were **semi-rigid**. A keel at the bottom of the canopy stopped it going out of shape. The top part was flexible, so that the gas pressure could be lower.

In 1670, Francesco de Lana Terzi designed this air-boat, which he hoped would sail through the air suspended from four copper spheres emptied of air.

The dirigible was steered by means of a rudder. A light engine drove the propeller. The weight of these parts was distributed along the whole length of the canopy by a long beam to which ropes were attached.

A propeller may be an air-screw, which pulls, or a true propeller, which pushes.

Early dirigibles

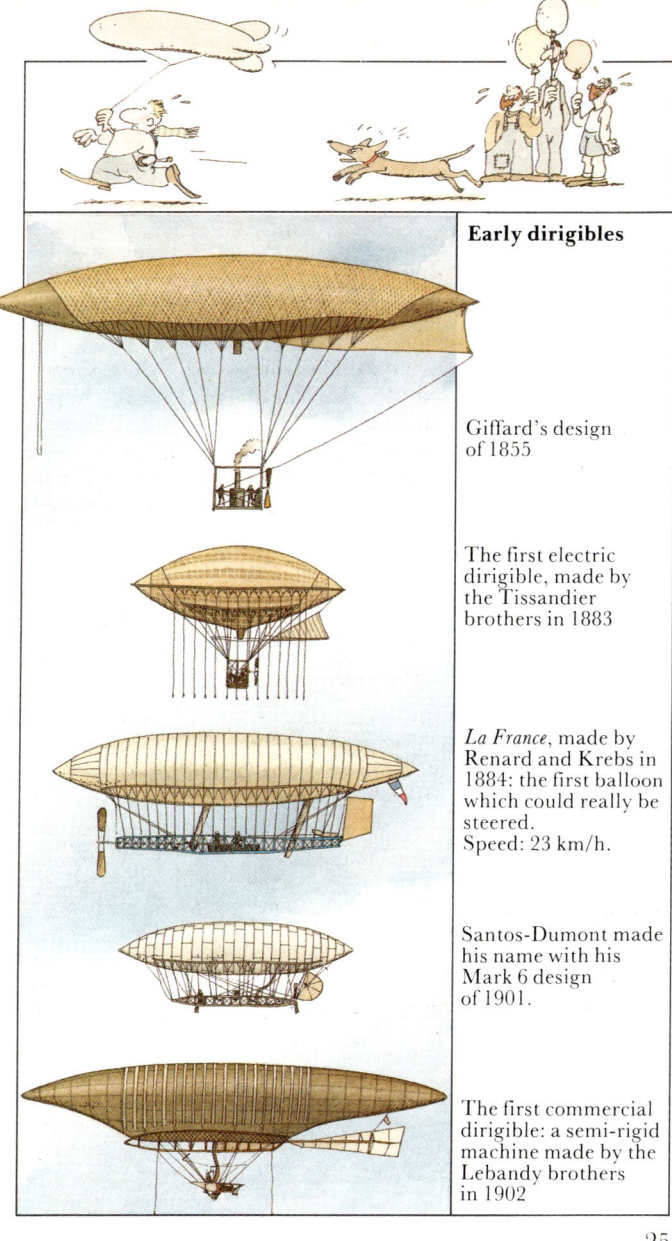

Giffard's design of 1855

The first electric dirigible, made by the Tissandier brothers in 1883

La France, made by Renard and Krebs in 1884: the first balloon which could really be steered.
Speed: 23 km/h.

Santos-Dumont made his name with his Mark 6 design of 1901.

The first commercial dirigible: a semi-rigid machine made by the Lebandy brothers in 1902

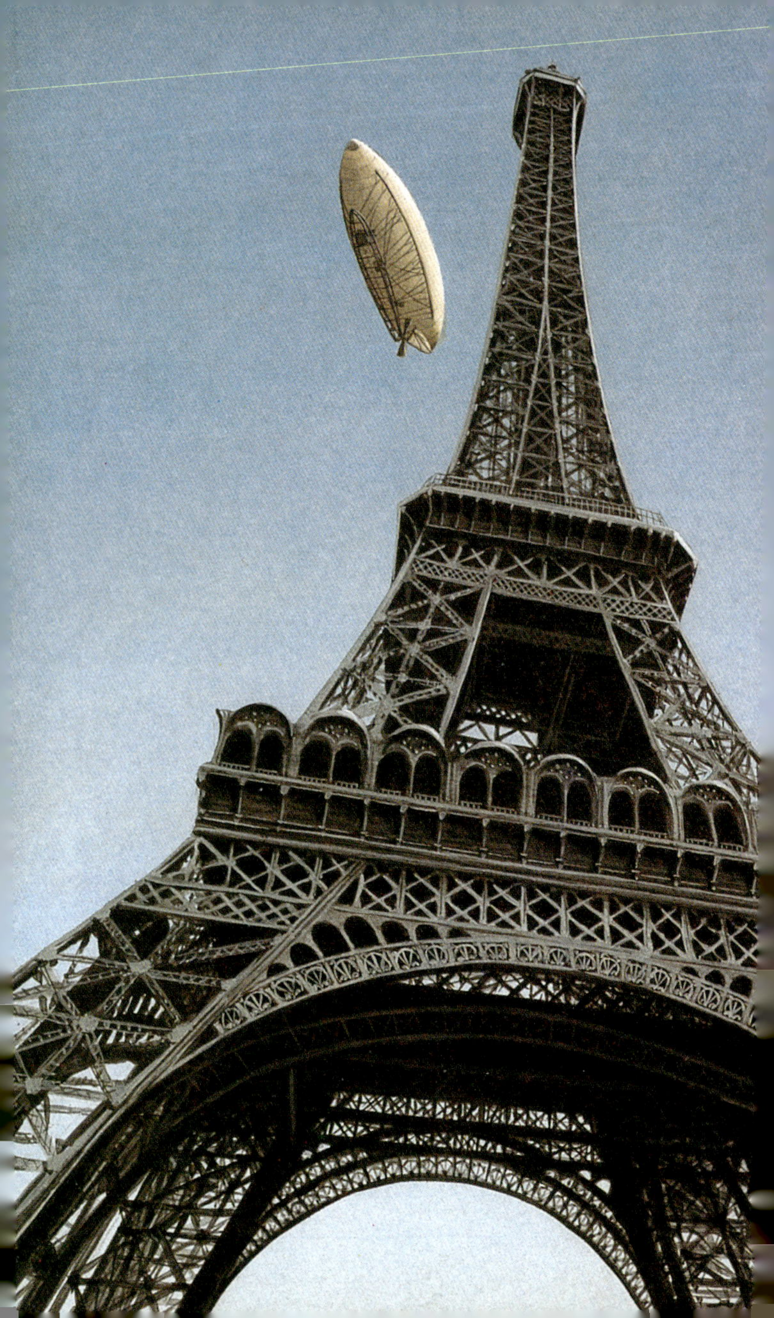

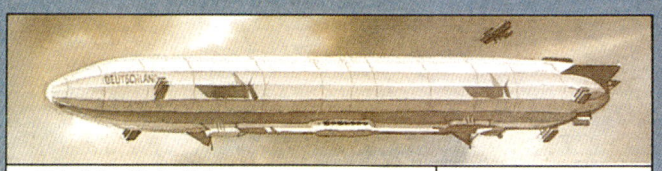

Rigid dirigibles were yet more impressively large. The cloth canopy was stretched over a metal skeleton, to which the gondolas and tail-fins were attached. Inside, the light gas was contained in small bags, called ballonets, distributed along the canopy.

Ferdinand von Zeppelin, a German count, presented his country with a whole fleet of rigid dirigibles. By 1918, 113 Zeppelins had been built. During the First World War the airships were used to bomb London and Paris at night. In peace-time, they transported both people and goods across the skies.

Alberto Santos-Dumont became famous on 17 October 1901: in his Mark 6 dirigible, he took off from St-Cloud, in Paris, flew round the Eiffel Tower, and returned to St-Cloud half an hour later. He won the prize of 100,000 francs which M. Deutsch de la Meurthe had offered in 1900.

A Zeppelin *LZ8* airship

Ferdinand von Zeppelin

Santos-Dumont, a rich Brazilian, settled in France in 1898 to work on airships. By 1907 he had built twelve flexible dirigibles.

Alberto Santos-Dumont

Sir George Cayley

George Cayley understood the different demands of propulsion and lift; he saw that the problem was to make the air support a surface bearing a given weight by using a driving force. Thus an aeroplane must have fixed wings to ensure that the machine has sufficient lift, so long as it is at the

George Cayley (1773-1857), a Yorkshireman, is often regarded as the father of air-navigation. From 1796 onwards he concentrated on the problem of flight, building small gliders which managed to fly.

He engraved on a silver disc a drawing of the first true aeroplane; on the back, he wrote down his ideas on the principles of flight.

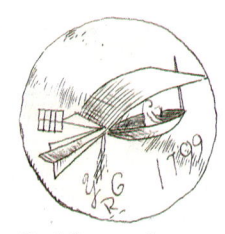

same time propelled forward at a sufficient speed. Stable flight is achieved if lift equals the weight of the aeroplane. If lift is greater than this, the aeroplane rises; if lift is less than this, the aeroplane falls.

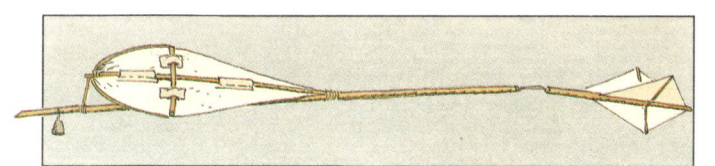

It became clear that Cayley was right when in 1849 a ten-year-old boy was carried several metres above the ground by a triplane travelling down a hill. In 1853, when he was eighty, Cayley ordered his coachman to get into the machine to try it again; he hoped to witness the first controlled flight by a machine that was heavier than air.

The *Kite-glider* of 1804, the first small-scale model Cayley succeeded in flying. It had a sloping fixed wing, and a cross-shaped tail to control horizontal and vertical steering. A movable weight provided balance so that the glider flew smoothly.

The *Manoeuvrable Parachute* of 1852. This glider had to be launched from a balloon.

Cayley's coachman flying in the glider. After a very bumpy ride to the bottom of the hill, the shaken coachman emerged and gave notice to his employer, saying that his job was to drive a coach, not to fly.

Heavier than air

Model aeroplane constructed in 1879 by Victor Tatin, a clock-maker. The motor was driven by compressed air.

In the second half of the 19th century, many people tried to imitate Cayley. They jumped out of balloons, they were pulled along by horses, they skidded down slopes; some achieved short gliding flights, while others broke their bones in their crazy machines. Only a few of their names are remembered: Le Bris, Pénaud, du Temple, Golubev, Montgomery...

During his voyages across the oceans,

Glider with feathered wings, made by Biot in 1879. To steer it, Biot put his feet in the stirrups, thus moving the tail.

Jean-Marie Le Bris, a captain in the French navy, studied the flight of the albatross. To find out more, he even killed one bird. In 1856 he built a machine, launched himself from a cart pulled by a galloping horse, and succeeded in rising 100 m into the air. At the second attempt, however, he broke his leg.

In 1856, Jean-Marie Le Bris made this glider, based on the wing-structure of the albatross.

In 1871 a naval engineer called Alphonse Penaud fitted a two-bladed propeller driven by twisted elastic on to a glider 50 cm long.

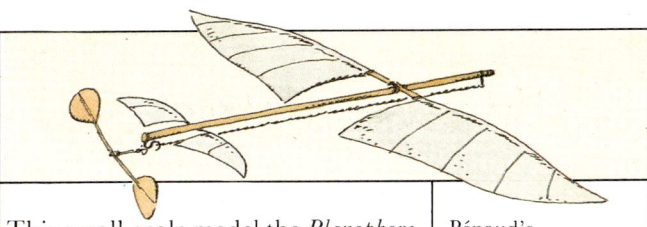

This small-scale model, the *Planophore*, was the first stable machine to fly; it travelled 60 m in 13 seconds.

Two men succeeded in taking off as their machines went down a slope, but they fell back to the ground almost at once. In 1874 Félix du Temple, another French naval officer, achieved the first take-off in a real aeroplane. A Russian, I. N. Golubev, repeated this exploit ten years later, in a steam monoplane devised by Alexander Mojaisky.

That same year, John Montgomery from California jumped out of a balloon, using his parachute-glider for the first time.

But so far, no one had invented an engine which could enable a machine heavier than air to take off; nor was there any kind of controlled flight.

Pénaud's *Planophore* (1871)

Alphonse Pénaud (1850-1880)

Félix du Temple taking off in 1874

Clément Ader

Clément Ader (1841-1925). His first design, built in 1873, was a glider made of goose-feathers, in which he managed to leave the ground.

Clément Ader worked on electricity and steam-engines, and was one of the pioneers of the telephone; from these activities, he made enough money to experiment with his ideas about flight.

A bat was the inspiration for his first aeroplane, which he named after Aeolus, the god of wind. On 9 October 1890 he managed to stay a few centimetres above the ground while travelling 50 metres. He was the first man to fly in a **machine powered by its own engine**.

Using money given to him by the French government, which was interested in the military possibilities of the scheme, Ader built the *Avion III*, and on 14 October 1897 he demonstrated his machine at an army camp. At 5.15 p.m., with the wind three-quarters behind it, the aeroplane gathered speed. The take-off was very weak, but suddenly a gust of wind caught the machine and lifted it from the runway. However, a committee decided that the trial was inconclusive, so the government withdrew its financial support, though Ader insisted that he had flown 300 m. He was so shattered by the decision that he set fire to his laboratory and all his papers.

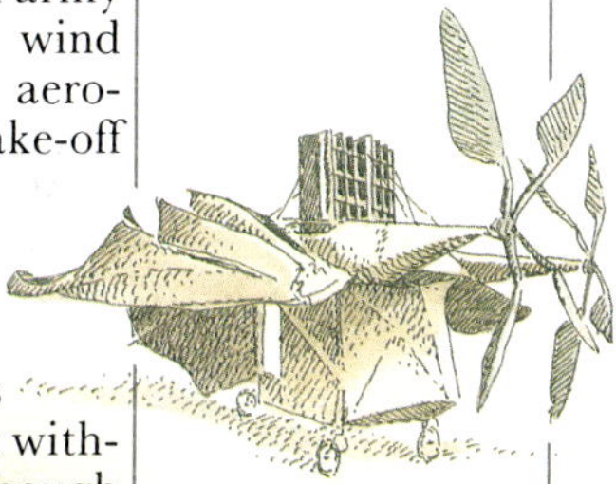

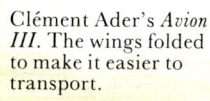

Clément Ader's *Avion III*. The wings folded to make it easier to transport.

Otto Lilienthal
The flying man

Lilienthal's reputation as the 'flying man' came from articles illustrated with photographs of him gliding; these appeared all over the world. Born in Germany on 24 May 1848, he was the first to realise that a pilot must control both his own body and his machine to achieve stability of flight. When he was a boy, he and his brother Gustav studied the way birds fly, and as early as 1860, the two boys were building rudimentary machines. Between 1891 and 1896 Otto built twelve monoplanes.

Otto Lilienthal studied physics and qualified as an engineer. After that he spent all his spare time doing experiments on the resistance of air, and on the relation between lift and the curvature of the wing.

In 1891 he built his first **glider** in the suburbs of Berlin. It was made of willow covered with cloth. He carried out trials in his garden, jumping first from a diving-board (up to 2.5 m high), then from the tops of mounds, then from the roof of his hangar (10 m above the ground), and finally from the top of a hill 15 m high, which he had built so that he could glide freely whatever the direction of the wind. During his public flights he managed to travel 200 to 300 m, at a speed of 10 m/sec., rising as high as 23 m.

'We must fly and fall... fly and fall... until we can fly without falling.' In five years, he carried out more than 2,000 gliding flights.

In 1896, as he was testing a biplane which was to contain an engine, he was thrown off balance by a gust of wind, and the glider broke up. He fell

Otto Lilienthal
(1848-1896)

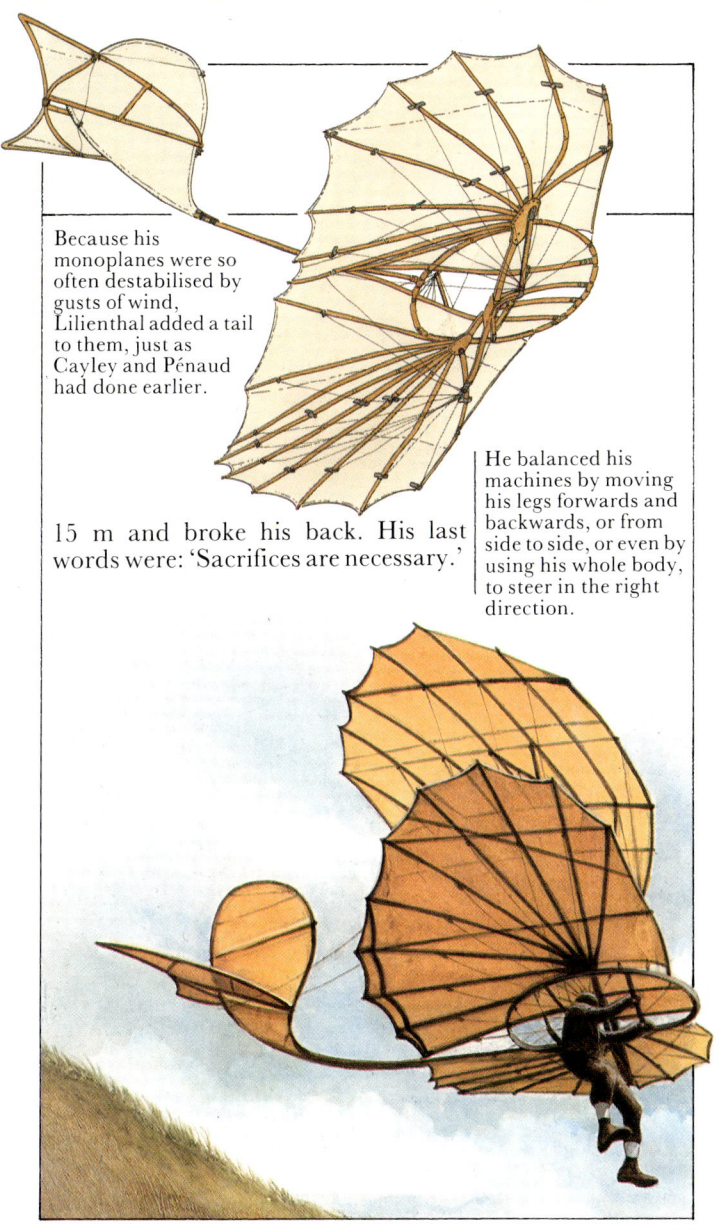

Because his monoplanes were so often destabilised by gusts of wind, Lilienthal added a tail to them, just as Cayley and Pénaud had done earlier.

15 m and broke his back. His last words were: 'Sacrifices are necessary.'

He balanced his machines by moving his legs forwards and backwards, or from side to side, or even by using his whole body, to steer in the right direction.

The dawn of the twentieth century

Pilcher (1866-1899) with his *Falcon*

Octavius Chanute (1832-1910)

Chanute's biplane glider

Percy Pilcher and Octavius Chanute continued Lilienthal's work.

Pilcher, a Scot, met Lilienthal in 1895, tried out his machines, and was inspired to build four gliders. The most successful was the *Falcon* (1896), which flew more than 200 m. Though it had an undercarriage, mounted on springs, this machine made use of many of Lilienthal's ideas. The pilot was suspended below the wings, and the tail was hinged so that it rose freely if a gust caught it from below; this prevented the machine from going into a nose-dive. During a demonstration flight on 30 September 1899, a tail-strut broke and the machine crashed. Pilcher was badly injured, and died two days later.

Chanute was an American railway engineer. In 1894, at the age of sixty-two, he wrote a book about the development of flying-machines. He was in touch with the pioneers of the period, and generously allowed them to use the fruits of his research.

In 1896 he began to build multi-wing gliders. His best design was a **two-winged glider**, with a cross-shaped tail; this was to have a direct influence on later craft.

Hiram Maxim, also an American, was an electrical engineer who moved to England in 1882 in order to devote himself to his new enthusiasm for flight. The result of his labours was a huge two-winged machine which could carry four passengers.

Maxim's enormous machine:
Surface area: 370 m^2
Wing-span: 31 m
Weight: 3.5 tonnes
2 steam-engines of 100 hp each
2 propellers, each 5.5 m in diameter
Trial flight: 1894, at Baldwyn's Park, Kent. The contraption ran on tracks, with guard-rails to prevent it from taking off out of control. The power of the engines enabled the biplane to reach a speed of 70 km/h., but as the machine rose it broke a guard-rail. Maxim had to stop the engines.
It had been an expensive trial.

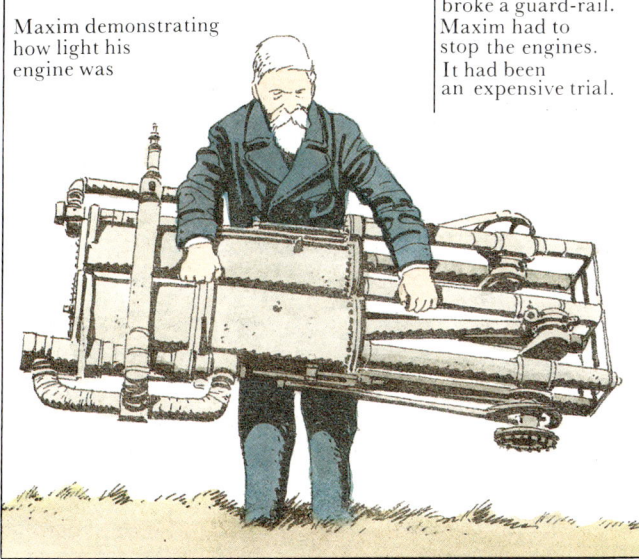

Maxim demonstrating how light his engine was

37

Samuel Langley's
Aerodrome

Professor Samuel Pierpont Langley (1834-1906), the secretary of America's most prestigious scientific society.

On the Potomac River in 1903: the *Aerodrome* is on its launching platform on top of the floating hangar.

Just before the Wright brothers' great exploit, everyone's attention was attracted by another American.

Samuel Pierpont Langley was not a crazy inventor, but a scientist and astronomer. He managed to get a small-scale model aircraft to fly more than a kilometre, launching it over the Potomac River by catapult. He called this aircraft, with its two pairs of curved wings, one behind the other, an 'aerodrome'.

In 1898, the US government offered him $50,000 to build a full-size piloted aircraft; they hoped that it would be useful to the army. In 1903 the *Aerodrome* was ready for testing over the Potomac. On 7 October the pilot, Manly, climbed in and the aircraft was catapulted from the roof of a barge. It immediately went into a nose-dive – straight into the river. The machine was not badly damaged and was recovered, ready for another attempt on 8 December. This time, when the machine was launched, the rear wings folded; the *Aerodrome* reared up and was ruined.

The government withdrew its support, and Langley, discouraged by the ridicule of the press, gave up his research.

The *Aerodrome* remained at the bottom of the Potomac until 1914, when it was rescued by Glenn Curtiss.

The Wright brothers

The Wright brothers were passionate inventors and makers of experimental machines, and flight was one of their interests. Lilienthal's death made them think again about the problem of heavier-than-air machines, and they decided that they would be the first to travel in a real aeroplane powered by a real engine.

They worked methodically, observing how birds flew and studying all the books and papers on aeronautics which Chanute sent them.

In order to carry out their experiments they decided to settle in a hut on a plot of land in Kitty Hawk, North Carolina, a small fishing village on the Atlantic coast, where there were large beaches and plenty of wind. That was where, on 17 December 1903, the *Flyer* brought them fame.

In 1902 Wilbur Wright discovered how to make his glider turn safely by banking.

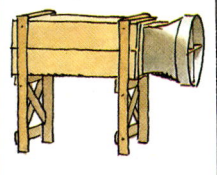

This wind-tunnel, perfected by the Wrights, enabled them to test different wing-shapes. From 1899 onwards they flew a succession of kites, gliders and aeroplanes.

Controlled flight

In 1905 the Wrights flew *Flyer III* for thirty-eight minutes, during which they travelled 39 km.

1 pitching
2 rolling
3 yawing

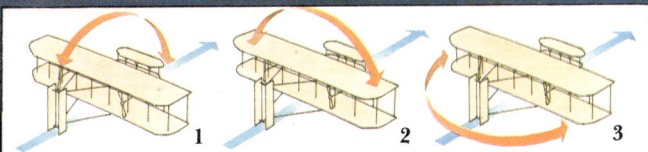

On 17 December 1903 it was cold, with a strong north-east wind. The aircraft, christened *Flyer*, was ready aboard a trailer, on the launching rail and facing into the wind.

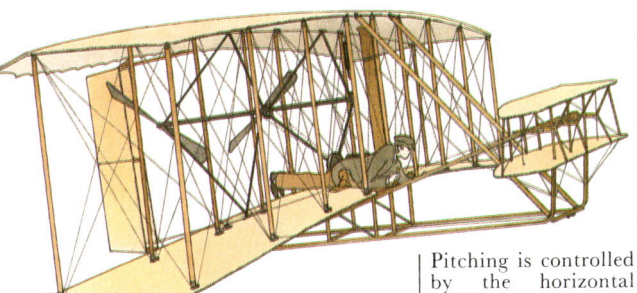

On the 1903 *Flyer* the pilot lay down, with his left hand on the mechanism to work the horizontal rudder; the other two controls were worked by his pelvis.

Pitching is controlled by the horizontal rudder, rolling by banking the wings, and yawing by the vertical rudder.

Who was to fly first? They tossed a coin, and Orville won. The flight lasted twelve seconds, and the aircraft travelled 36 m.

The *Flyer* flew four times that day, the two brothers taking turns at the controls. The fourth flight was the longest: 260 m in 59 seconds. Altogether they had achieved 98 seconds of controlled flight, thus triumphantly achieving their goal. They were the first people in the world **to fly in an aeroplane which they really controlled**.

Orville   Wilbur

Santos-Dumont and Ferber

In Europe at the beginning of this century, aeroplanes were overshadowed by the success of airships until the Brazilian Santos-Dumont reawakened public interest in heavier-than-air machines.

'My name is Santos, and I weigh 41 kg without my shoes (but with my gloves).' This was how Alberto Santos-Dumont introduced himself. Already the talk of Paris for his airship exploits, he increased his popularity by making the **first properly recorded European flight** in an aeroplane with an engine, on 12 November 1906. He travelled 220 m in 21 seconds (41 km/h), to win another Deutsch de la Meurthe prize, this time for being the first person to fly more than 50 m in a straight line.

Santos-Dumont's *XIVa* looked very strange. It was shaped like a duck

The transition from airship to aeroplane: in 1906 Santos-Dumont tested the controls of his *XIVa* while it was tethered below his airship *No. 14*.

The Demoiselle

and made of boxes, like Hargrave's kite. One box, at the end of a long neck, controlled the steering. And as if to emphasise the pilot's eccentricity, the machine flew backwards, because the engine drove a true propeller, not an air-screw. It could only travel 220 m but Santos-Dumont did not give up; he built a series of beautiful little monoplanes, based on his famous *Demoiselle* of 1908, a design which was as well-loved as its designer.

Before Santos-Dumont, the Frenchman Captain Ferdinand Ferber was the best-known European pioneer of flight.

In 1898, much influenced by Lilienthal, he began making gliders. In 1901 he flew 15m.

He studied the work of his friend, Octavius Chanute, as well as that of the Wright brothers. He too built an aircraft with an engine, and worked out a system for learning to fly by attaching his aeroplane to a crane, so that he could always turn the aircraft's nose into the wind; this was the first flight simulator.

With his Mark 6 machine he achieved stability by arranging the wings so that they formed an arrow when seen from above (1), a V seen from in front (2), and an angle with the axis of the rear of the aircraft when seen from the side (3).

He flew his Mark 8 machine in 1908.

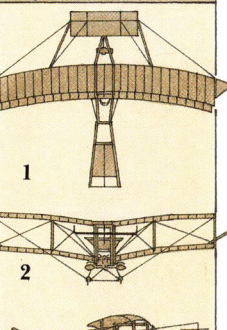

Ferber's Mark 6

Captain Ferdinand Ferber (1862-1909)

The first European flights

Trojan Vuia's aircraft (1906)

Just before the Wright brothers' great success, Karl Jatho, from Germany, managed to make several short flights; his best effort was an uncontrolled leap of 60 m.

In 1905 Trojan Vuia, a Hungarian engineer, settled in France. He designed a machine which looked like a car with wings and a propeller; it was steered by the front wheels. He had the machine built, and in 1907 it flew 24 m. But without controls the craft became unstable and crashed. Vuia gave up flight and concentrated on cars instead.

In Denmark, Jacob Ellehammer managed to leap 40 m in an aircraft which he built entirely on his own.

Cody at the 1903 Exhibition in the Alexandra Palace, London

Samuel Franklin Cody was a real-life cowboy from the Wild West, and a famous conjurer. He was a contemporary of William F. Cody (Buffalo Bill), but they were not related.

In 1890 Cody moved to England, and first took an interest in kites, which he would fly, wearing a cowboy costume, for anyone who wanted to watch.

He made the **first officially recorded flight in Britain** (424 m) on 16 October 1908, in an aircraft which he had built for the army. This feat took place at **Farnborough**, which has since become one of the best-known airfields in Britain.

Cody in his aeroplane, the *Cathedral*, in 1909

This small monoplane, rather like the *Demoiselle*, was built by the German Hans Grade in 1909.

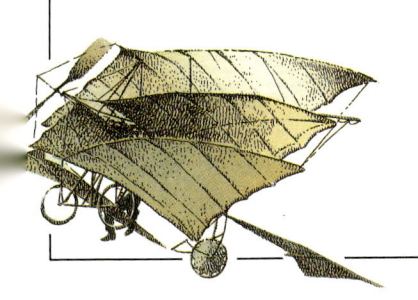

Ellehammer and his triplane (1908)

47

Propellers and engines

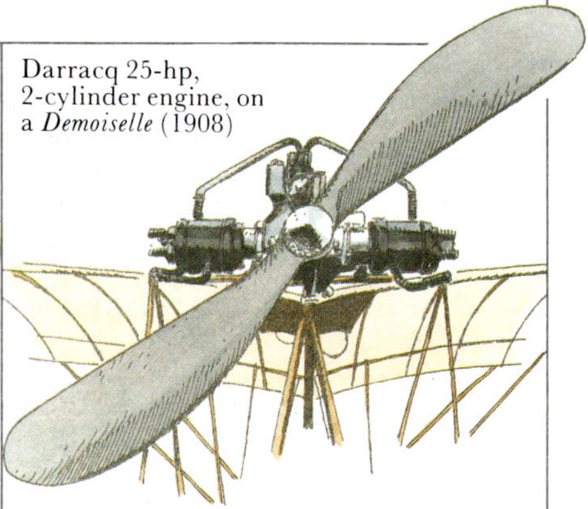

Darracq 25-hp, 2-cylinder engine, on a *Demoiselle* (1908)

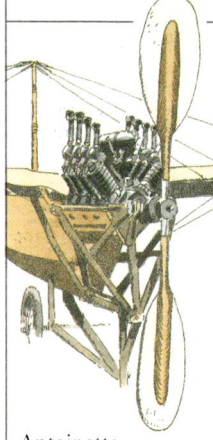

Antoinette engine (1908), 50 hp, V8

Ernest Archdeacon's flying-motor-bike shows how effective the propeller is as a means of propulsion. It reached a speed of 80 km/h.

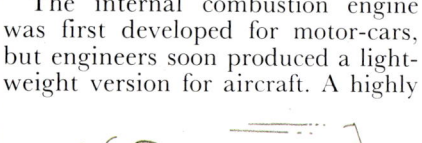

The ancestors of propellers were the great sails of windmills; the first aircraft propellers even looked a bit like them. But they worked differently. The wind moves the mill sails, which in turn move the machinery; a propeller is driven by the engine and makes the aeroplane move through the air.

The internal combustion engine was first developed for motor-cars, but engineers soon produced a lightweight version for aircraft. A highly inflammable mixture of air and fuel is injected into the cylinder, and ignited by a spark. The resultant explosion pushes the piston, which is joined by a rod to the crankshaft. The piston moves in a straight line; the rod transforms this movement into the rotary movement of the crankshaft; the crankshaft turns the propeller.

The cylinders can be arranged around the crankshaft in different ways, lined up horizontally, or in a V or W shape.

When the aircraft flies, the force of the engine and propeller provides 'thrust', and the resistance opposing this is 'drag'. If thrust and drag are equal, the aircraft flies at a constant speed. If thrust is greater, it accelerates; if drag is greater, it slows down.

The 'chariot-automobile' which Captain Ferber built in 1906 to study how propellers work

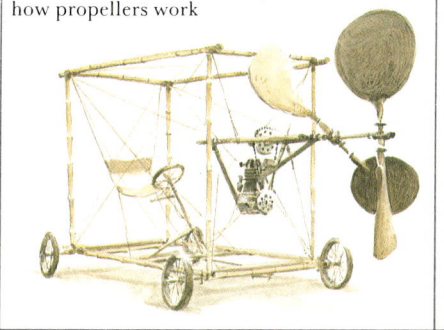

A 1912 *Blériot* had no brakes, so it had to be held down on the ground when the engine was running.

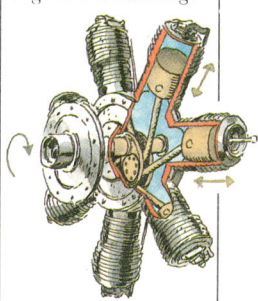

The famous Gnome engine made by the Seguin brothers in 1908, 50 hp, 7 cylinders in a star

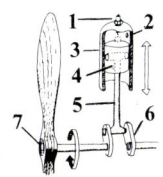

1 Spark plug
2 Fuel-injection nozzle
3 Cylinder
4 Piston
5 Piston-rod
6 Crankshaft
7 Propeller-shaft

The power of an engine is measured in horse-power (hp).

49

The plane-makers

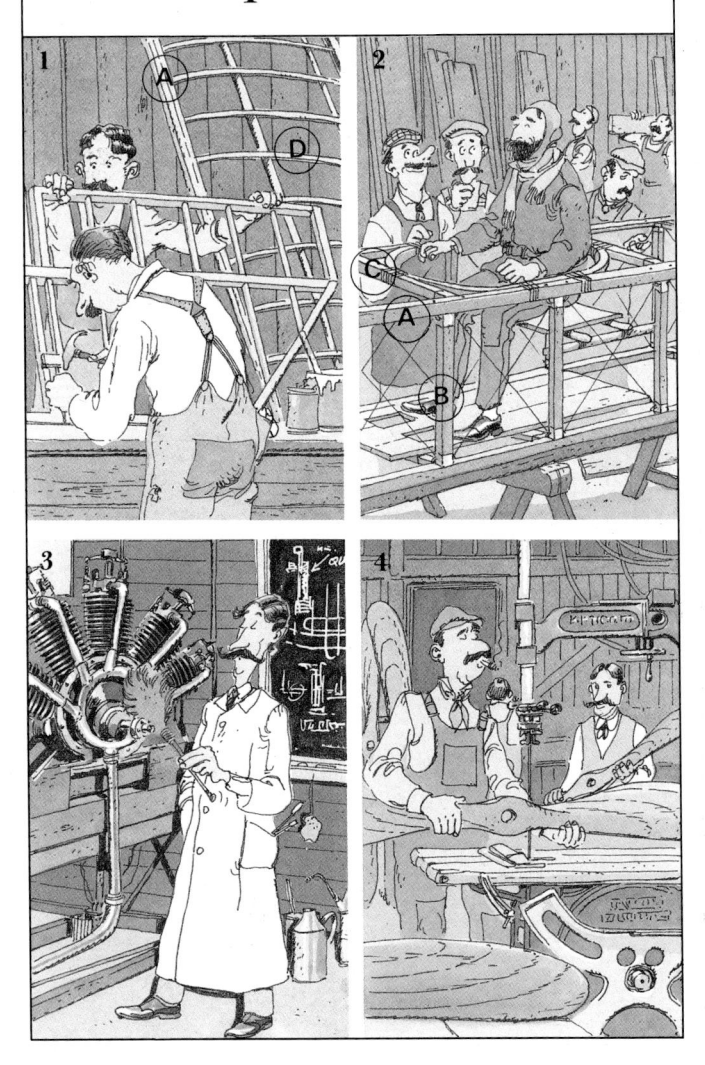

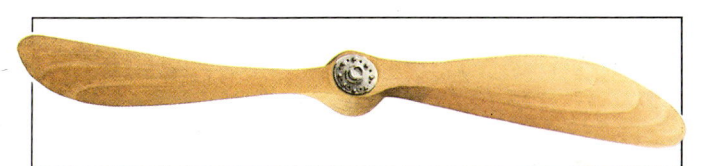

Most early aircraft were built of bamboo. It was light, rigid, needed no shaping, and was cheap. The bamboo rods were fixed together with small pieces of metal, and the whole structure was held rigid by a criss-cross arrangement of metal cables. Later on, timber (pine, ash or birch) replaced bamboo, as it was better for making more sophisticated wings.

The pictures opposite show the stages of the plane's construction. Four curved longerons (A) formed the framework of the fuselage. They were usually linked vertically by uprights (B), and horizontally by cross-pieces (C). The outer surfaces were covered with cloth, generally varnished silk or proofed linen. The wings were built round one or two longerons which could stand the stress of twisting and bending. Ribs (D) were attached at right-angles to the basic framework.

From 1909 propellers were made of hardwood, with the grain running lengthways to resist the centrifugal force.

Some designers tried new shapes. The results were not always convincing!

Léon Levavasseur (1863-1922), a former artist, he built the famous Antoinette engine in 1907, as well as the aeroplane of the same name in which Hubert Latham broke the altitude record (155 m) at Reims in 1909.

In the first aircraft workshops, craftsmen shaped the wooden parts, assembled the fuselage and the wings (1), then added the wires (2). The engine was adjusted (3) and the propeller was made (4). All this in an atmosphere reeking of glue and castor oil.

The beginning of the aircraft industry

The Voisin brothers, Charles (1884-1912) and Gabriel (1880-1974), in their workshop at Billancourt

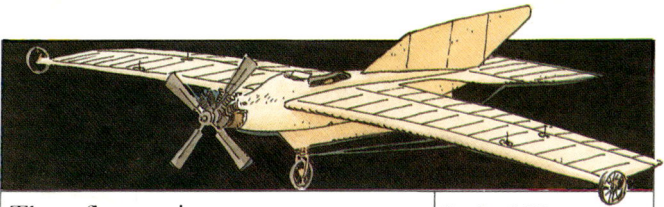

The first aviators were master-craftsmen who made their own aircraft and engines. They had to be designers and builders as well as pilots.

After 1907, changes came rapidly. Flight could now be controlled, and there were two light and reliable engines, the Antoinette (1907) and the Gnome (1908).

Encouraged by all these successes, some aviators decided to start building aircraft for other people. The largest workshops were those of the Voisin brothers, Levassen, Bleriot and Farman in France, and the Wright brothers and Curtiss in America. Theirs were the first aircraft factories.

In the *REP*, designed by Robert Esnault-Pelterie in 1907, all the controls were worked by a single lever, the 'joystick'.

Mark 6

Mark 7

Two monoplanes made by Louis Blériot in 1907

On 13 January 1908 the *Voisin*, with an Antoinette engine, was flown by Henri Farman to win the Deutsch-Archdeacon prize for the first flight round a 1 km circuit.

Helicopters

A sycamore seed

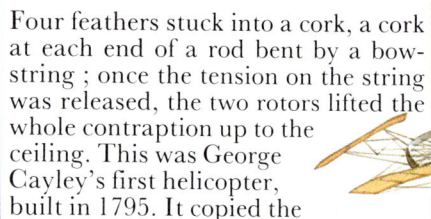

Four feathers stuck into a cork, a cork at each end of a rod bent by a bowstring; once the tension on the string was released, the two rotors lifted the whole contraption up to the ceiling. This was George Cayley's first helicopter, built in 1795. It copied the ideas suggested by the French engineers Launoy and Bienvenue a year earlier, though in fact it was Leonardo da Vinci who first dreamed up the helicopter.

In 1843 Cayley designed the *Pigeon*, a machine capable of vertical take-off; for this it had two pairs of rotors. It

George Cayley's *Pigeon* (1843)

Leonardo da Vinci's 'aerial screw' or 'helicopter', inspired by Archimedes' screw

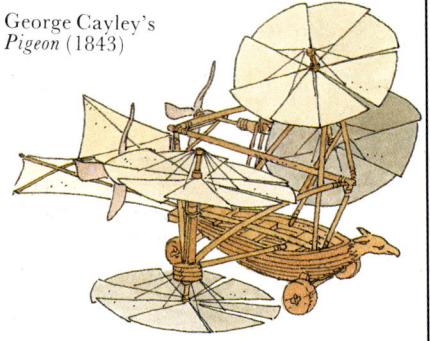

also had two conventional propellers. Lift and balance were provided by the blades of the rotors, which pivoted to form four umbrella-shaped wings.

In the earliest days of aviation, taking off in a fixed-wing aircraft and landing it again was very tricky. Some people thought that vertical take-off was the answer to the problem.

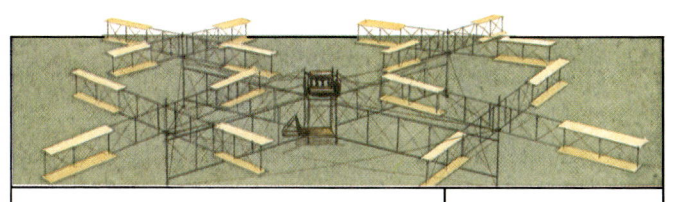

The *Gyroplane* built by Bréguet and Richet in 1907

Paul Cornu's helicopter (1907)

The famous Antoinette engines were used in the first two attempts. On 29 September 1907, in Douai, Bréguet and Richet's *Gyroplane* rose, with a pilot on board, and stayed 1.5 m above the ground for over a minute. Admittedly, the machine was held fast by cables to avoid accidents. A few weeks later, on 13 November, Paul Cornu made the **first free helicopter flight** at Lisieux: 30 seconds, at a height of 1.5 m.

Louis Vuitton's helicopter of 1910 never progressed beyond the design stage.

I reckon that if a machine fitted with a rotor is properly made, using material whose pores have been sealed with starch, and if the rotor is then turned quickly, it will describe a spiral and raise the whole machine into the air.
Leonardo da Vinci

Crossing the Channel

Hubert Latham's plane was the *Antoinette*, designed by Levavasseur.
Wing span: 12.8 m
Length: 11.7 m
Total weight: 500 kg
Engine: Antoinette, 50 hp

The *Blériot XI*, Louis Blériot's machine.
Wing span: 8.6 m
Length: 7.8 m
Total weight: 300 kg
Engine: Anzani, 25 hp

In the summer of 1909, two Frenchmen were competing to be first to fly across the Channel. Hubert Latham took off first, leaving Sangatte on 19 July. The weather was good. But ten minutes later, the engine stalled at 300 m, and the *Antoinette* fell into the sea.

As Latham was planning another attempt, Blériot was waiting for fine weather. On 25 July he took off from

Barraques, and flew over Cap Blanc-Nez. Half an hour later, near Dover, a village policeman happened to look

Louis Blériot

up. 'I saw what looked like a huge butterfly flying in the sky. I rang the police station, then ran as fast as I could. I met the aviator in the meadow, and he shook my hand in both of his. It was wonderful!'

Latham, wet, cold and bitterly disappointed, sits on the floating wreckage of his plane and waits for rescue.

The English Channel

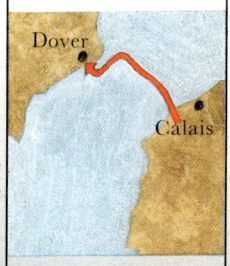

Blériot's Channel crossing: the first international flight

Sea-planes

Gabriel Voisin taking off from the River Seine on 8 June 1905, in the biplane *Archdeacon* towed by a motor-boat

Henri Fabre's sea-plane, the *Hydravion*, was the first aircraft to take off from the surface of the water, on 28 March 1910.

A.V. Roe (1877-1958), an English designer, built this *Avro* in 1911.

The first person to try to take off from water was Wilhelm Kress, an Austrian piano-builder. In 1901, at the age of 65, he climbed into an aeroplane of his own design. It had a double shell made of aluminium, three pairs of wings, one behind the other, and two propellers driven by a Daimler 30-hp petrol-engine. As he prepared to take off, he had to swerve to avoid an obstacle; the machine overturned and sank, and Kress abandoned the idea.

In 1909 and 1910 other people, including Blériot, the Voisins and the Wrights, tried to solve the problem. The best known was Glenn Curtiss, an American. He built the first really specialised sea-plane, with a central float on the fuselage and a stabiliser at the end of each wing. This machine, developed from his propeller biplane of 1909, flew on 26 January 1911. In 1912 he completed a new design: a sea-plane with a central hull which held the pilot and all the controls.

Langley's *Aerodrome*, modified by Curtiss and flown by him in 1914 on Lake Kenka, in New York State

Curtiss A-1 (1911)

Glenn H. Curtiss
(1878-1930)

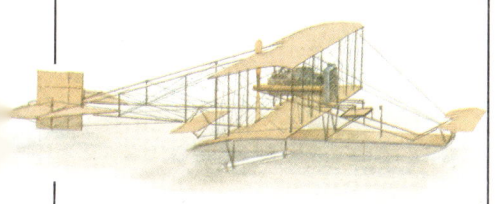

Flights in public

On 28 March 1908 Léon Delagrange, a French sculptor, tried to take Henry Farman on a flight in his *Voisin*, but the aircraft could not take off laden with the weight of two men.

From 1908 onwards, progress was rapid. Flying became a practical proposition, and people began to think of it as a means of transport.

Wilbur Wright started a flying school in Pau in 1909. He gave flying lessons to Alfonso XIII, King of Spain, who was an enthusiast.

On 13 January Henri Farman flew over a 200 m course between two poles. On 30 May he took off from Ghent with the **world's first air-passenger**, Ernest Archdeacon. They flew 1,241 m.

On 8 July, in Turin, Delagrange succeeded in flying 200 m, at a height of 5 m, accompanied by Thérèse Peltier, the first woman air-passenger.

In July Wilbur Wright settled in France, at Le Mans, and tried to make his *Flyer* commercially viable. He offered rides to passengers, and gave demonstration flights. By the end of the year he held all the world records

In America, on 4 July 1908, Curtiss made the first public flight of more than one kilometre, flying his *June Bug*.

Was it because of aviation that narrow skirts became fashionable?

for flying (duration, altitude – 120 m – and distance), but he flew only over a special course.

On 30 October Farman made the **first real journey by air**: Bouy to Reims, 27 km at 75 km/h, at a height of 25 m.

Pilots wanted to practise their skills, and many people were eager to learn to fly. Flying schools and aerodromes were set up, and from the end of 1908 a pilot had to pass a test.

Laws were passed to govern flying. If a pilot landed just anywhere, he was liable to be fined.

61

Airshows

The first great international airshow, at Reims in 1909

To demonstrate feats of aviation to a wider public, airshows were organised. The first were held in France, but the idea soon caught on elsewhere. These gatherings provided an opportunity for aviators, famous or not so

Etevé speedometer

The air pressure generated by the speed of the aircraft moves the block of wood. The red mark shows the normal speed. If the needle is above the mark, the aeroplane is flying dangerously fast; if it falls below, the aircraft is losing speed and may crash.

famous, to test their skills. Some of them flew as private individuals; others were employed by manufacturers, who used these occasions to compete against one another.

The Reims airshow lasted a week in August 1909. More than forty pilots entered to compete for the large prizes offered by the local champagne firms, but only thirty-four turned up, and only eighteen of these (fifteen French, and one each from Britain, Spain and the USA) made a successful qualifying flight. Curtiss, the American, won the Gordon-Bennet cup for the fastest flight (73.637 km/h) twice round a 10-km course. Blériot won the prize for the fastest single lap (76.995 km/h). The endurance prize went to Farman (180 km); he also won the prize for a flight with a passenger. Latham won the altitude prize by reaching 155 m.

James Gordon-Bennet was a great patron of sport. He financed expeditions, he donated prizes for motor-races, boat-races and balloon-races, and he gave the most valuable prize at the Reims airshow.

1 *Farman* (biplane)
2 *Blériot* (monoplane)
3 *Curtiss* (biplane)
4 *Wright* (biplane)
5 *Voisin* (biplane)
6 *Antoinette* (monoplane)

Air-races

A.V. Roe's *Avro F* (1912). For the first time, the pilot is enclosed in an aluminium cabin.

The aircraft which attracted attention at airshows were very different from those built by the Wright brothers. Designs developed amazingly fast, especially in France where there were twelve competing manufacturers. If a firm wanted to sell its products abroad, it had to court publicity, and the best way to do that was by winning a race.

Everyone was crazy about aircraft. The first air-races took place in 1910. To start with they were held in a single country: London to Manchester, or St Petersburg to Moscow, or the six-day race held in eastern France in August that year.

Jules Védrines (1881-1919) won the Paris to Madrid race in 1911. The journey took him fourteen hours, at an average speed of 120 km/h.

Later they were international: Paris to Madrid, or Paris to Rome. Finally, in June 1911, came the circuit of Europe. This was flown in stages, over a total distance of 1,650 km.

At this stage, there was **no system of aerial navigation**. It was all just an adventure, and plenty of pilots got lost in the countryside. In addition, the engines kept breaking down. It became impossibly expensive to run the rescue service, so people gave up having races and went back to organising airshows. All the 1909 records were broken; in 1913 the altitude record was 5,900 m, and the speed record was 200.5 km/h.

The *Déperdussin* about to take off: once the engine is running, the ground staff have to hold the aircraft down on the ground until the pilot tells them to let go.

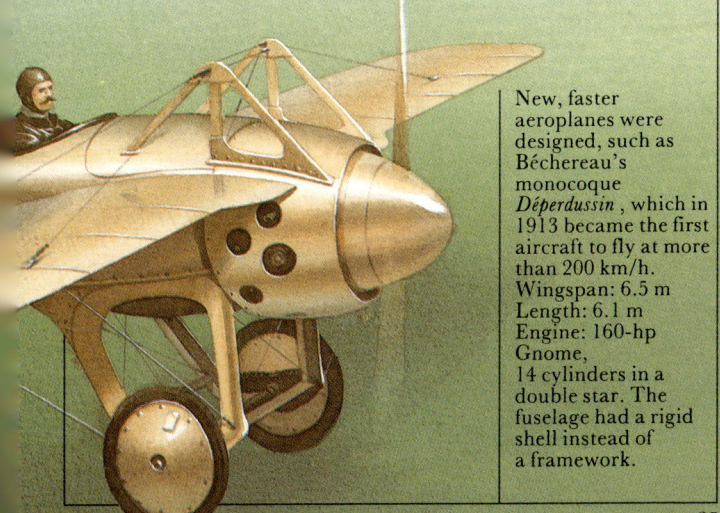

New, faster aeroplanes were designed, such as Béchereau's monocoque *Déperdussin*, which in 1913 became the first aircraft to fly at more than 200 km/h.
Wingspan: 6.5 m
Length: 6.1 m
Engine: 160-hp Gnome,
14 cylinders in a double star. The fuselage had a rigid shell instead of a framework.

65

Long-distance flights

George Chavez (1887-1910) came from Peru. He was killed when he crash-landed his *Blériot* at Domodossola, in Italy, just after his flight across the Alps on 23 September 1910.

Once aeroplanes could travel faster than trains, nothing could stop the progress of air transport.

In 1910 Charles Rolls, of Rolls-Royce, managed to fly across the Channel both ways without stopping; T.O.M. Sopwith flew 270 km from Kent to Belgium; Claude Grahame-White made the first night flight, during the London to Manchester race.

In 1911 Calbraith P. Rodgers flew across the USA from east to west, a journey which took him forty-nine days and which he did in eighty-two stages; Pierre Prier made the first non-stop flight from Paris to London; the first postal flight took place in India.

In 1912 Harriet Quimby, an American, became the first woman to fly across the Channel.

Crossing the Mediterranean

Early in the morning of 23 September 1913, Roland Garros filled the tanks of his *Morane-Saulnier* with 150 litres of fuel, put on his life-jacket, clambered into the cockpit, and took off from Fréjus, on France's south coast, at 5.47 a.m. bound for Tunis on the other side of the Mediterranean.

But as he flew over Sardinia, 'suddenly, an alarming sound of shattering metal; the whole machine shuddered... there was a bulge in the engine cowling, and black oil oozed out where the sheet metal had been pierced. The wind blew the oil into my face.' Nonetheless, the engine was still running. Garros hesitated: 'If I landed, I should ruin the flight; it would be the end of a dream.' Courageously, he flew on, and landed at Bizerte after 7 hours and 35 minutes in the air, with only 5 litres of fuel left in his tanks.

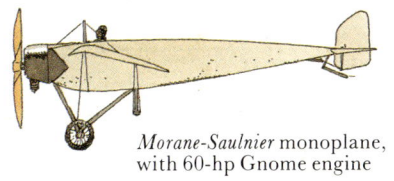

Roland Garros
(1888-1918)

Morane-Saulnier monoplane, with 60-hp Gnome engine

The route taken by Garros across the Mediterranean

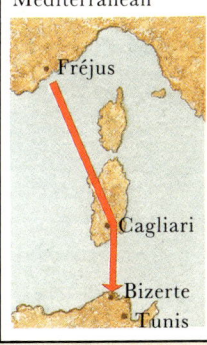

On the eve of the First World War

In 1909 the first international exhibition of air transport took place in the Grand Palais in Paris. There were 333 exhibitors, all but fifteen of them French. The general public came to admire; businessmen came to see whether the new means of transport was likely to be a profitable investment.

But flying was not yet safe. There were plenty of accidents, some of them fatal; thirty-two pilots were killed in 1910 alone.

Some safety-measures became standard. Pilots wore seat-belts so that they could not be knocked out of the aircraft if it was affected by turbulence, and they also wore flying-helmets. In 1912 **parachutes began to be used as a means of escaping** from a crashing aircraft.

The whole technique of flying became much more sophisticated, thanks to the efforts of dare-devil pilots who risked their necks.

One of these was Adolphe Pégoud, who in 1913 flew his aeroplane upside-down for 500 metres. He was also the first man to loop the loop, and devised a whole series of fantastic manoeuvres in the air; he invented what we now call **aerobatics**.

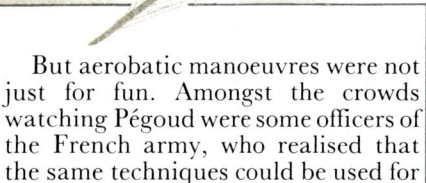

But aerobatic manoeuvres were not just for fun. Amongst the crowds watching Pégoud were some officers of the French army, who realised that the same techniques could be used for fighting in the air.

Although some of the army believed that aircraft had a future as military weapons, others were sceptical. Marshal Foch, for instance, said, 'It's just a sport; as far as the Army's concerned, aviation is useless.' An official military committee thought much the same: 'Let them amuse themselves by flying, so long as they don't frighten the horses.'

Adolphe Pégoud (1889-1915). The idea of aerobatics came to him in 1913, when he abandoned a *Blériot* to try a parachute-jump.

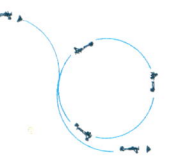

Looping the loop, a manoeuvre invented by Adolphe Pégoud. Many other manoeuvres have been invented since then: the horizontal eight (a figure-of-eight), the rolling circle, the stall turn, the spin, the horizontal slow roll. Aerobatic displays are now a regular feature of airshows.

An A to Z of aircraft facts

Aero-
This prefix comes from the Greek word for 'air', and was much used by the pioneers of flight when naming their machines.

Aerobatics
Acrobatics in the air

Aerodynamic
An aerodynamic shape is designed to cut wind-resistance to the absolute minimum.

Aeronaut
A balloonist.

Aeronautics
The science of flight. It includes the design and the building of all sorts of aircraft, both aeroplanes and other flying-machines, as well as the study of the skills needed to fly them efficiently.

Aerostat
An early name for a balloon or airship; a lighter-than-air flying-machine.

Aileron
A hinged surface on the trailing edge of the wing. It is used to steer the aeroplane, and enables it to turn in the air.

Altitude
Height above the ground.

Alula
Part of bird's wing; it provides stability in flight.

Aviator
The pilot of an early aeroplane; the word comes from the Latin for 'bird'.

Ballast
Extra weight, usually bags of sand, carried in a balloon; it can be jettisoned in order to make the balloon lighter.

Balloon
Balloons can be either captive (i.e. tethered to the ground) or free. Barrage balloons, and balloons used for various kinds of observation, are captive; most other balloons are free.

Banking
Making an aeroplane turn in the air. In early aircraft there were no ailerons. In order to turn the aircraft, the pilot had to twist the ends of the wings by pulling on a cable, rather like a rider using the reins to make his horse change direction.

Biplane
A biplane has two pairs of fixed wings, one pair above the other.

70

Castor oil
This was used to lubricate aircraft engines. It was added directly to the fuel and was carried right into the engine, so that there was no need for a separate lubrication system.

Charles, Jacques (1746-1823)
Designed and constructed the first hydrogen balloon. On 27 August 1783 his balloon, which was named the *Charlière* after its inventor, flew from Paris to Gonesse, 25 km away; at Gonesse the balloon was attacked by the local people when it fell from the sky.

Cockpit
The part of the aircraft where the pilot sits. The first aircraft had no cockpit; the pilot was just strapped on below the wings.

Cruciform
A cruciform tail is shaped like a cross. The horizontal part of the cross controls altitude, while the vertical part acts as a rudder to control the direction in which the aeroplane flies.

Cylinder
A cylindrical tube in the engine; it contains a piston.

Dirigible
The name means 'able to be steered'. A balloon is at the mercy of the wind; the pilot has some control over altitude, but none over direction. A dirigible has a propeller, which gives the pilot rather more control.

Drag
The resistance which an aircraft offers to the air.

Edge
A wing has two edges. The leading edge, at the front, cuts through the air, which then slides over the trailing edge at the back. The shape of the two wing-edges affects the aerodynamic efficiency of the aircraft.

Elevator
The rudder which controls altitude is known as the elevator.

71

Fuselage
The body of an aircraft.

Gas
At first, hot air was used to inflate balloons, but this was dangerous because it involved having a fire just at the base of the canopy. Then hydrogen was used. It was lighter, which made flying easier, but it was expensive. In the 19th century, they tried coal-gas, which was cheap and easy to obtain. Unfortunately both hydrogen and coal-gas are highly inflammable. Balloonists today use helium, which is inert.

Glider
A glider is an aircraft which has no engine; to take off it is towed, either by a land vehicle or by a conventional aeroplane. Once in the air, it flies by using the lift provided by upward air-currents, or thermals. These are the currents which some birds use when they soar.

Ground crew
These were a vital part of the teams which enabled the early aviators to fly. As well as preparing the aircraft and ensuring that everything was working correctly, they had to be prepared to hold the machine down until the pilot was ready to fly.

Helicopter
A type of aircraft without conventional wings. Instead it has one or more rotors, large horizontal propellers whose action lifts the helicopter into the air. A helicopter can take off vertically; it does not need a runway. This means that helicopters can be used in places where it would be impossible for a conventional aircraft to take off or land.

Hovering
Flying at a constant height without moving through the air. Some birds, such as kestrels, can do this; so can helicopters. Other aircraft cannot.

Hull
The hull of an aeroplane (or of a seaplane or boat) is the main or central part of its body.

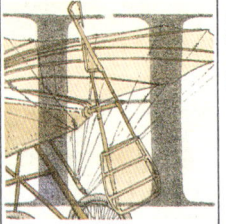

Hydrogen
The lightest of all gases, used to inflate early balloons from about 1790. It was extracted from water (H_2O) by forcing water vapour through a tube which also contained hot iron.

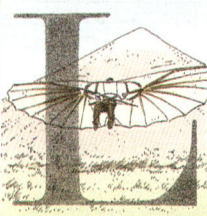

Lift
Lift is the upward pressure from the air which enables an aircraft to take off from the ground.

Monocoque
A monocoque aircraft has a fuselage whose outside shell is a strong part of its structure. Earlier aircraft had a rigid framework, and the outside was simply a cover. The French word *coque* means 'eggshell'.

Monoplane
A monoplane is an aircraft which has only one pair of wings. Most modern aircraft are monoplanes.

Montgolfière
This was a balloon named after the Montgolfier brothers. It was filled with air heated by a burner at the base of the balloon.

Nacelle
The basket, or gondola, below a balloon or airship. The pilot and any passengers sit there.

Ornithopter
Aircraft with moving wings. The name comes from the Greek for 'bird' and 'wing'.

Piston
Cylindrical part of the engine; it is moved in its cylinder by the force of the fuel explosion, and transmits this movement through the pistol-rod to the crankshaft.

Propeller
A wing which is twisted across the middle. When it is driven by the engine, it makes the aircraft move through the air. The propeller can be an airscrew, which pulls, at the front of the engine, or a true propeller, which pushes, at the rear. The first propellers were made of wood covered in cloth; they were rounded wooden plates fixed on spars. The first modern propellers were made in 1909.

Reims
A city in the champagne-making region of France, about 135 km north-east of Paris. The first great airshow was held there in 1909.

Rolling
One of the three movements of an aircraft. Rolling is the rotation of the fuselage, caused by one wing-tip being higher than the other.

Rudder
A device for controlling the direction, vertical or horizontal, in which an aircraft flies.

Simulator
A device used to teach flying skills while still safely on the ground. There is a complete set of controls and the learner can practise using them before taking to the air.

Span
The wing-span of an aircraft is the distance from the tip of one wing to the tip of the other.

Sustentation
The way in which an aeroplane remains airborne. It is achieved by a combination of thrust from the engine and lift from the air.

Smithsonian
James Smithson, an 18th-century British inventor and friend of Jacques Charles, inspired the Smithsonian Institution and the now world-famous Smithsonian's National Air and Space Museum in Washington, worth a visit to the USA!

Vertical take-off
Taking off by rising vertically into the air, as a helicopter does, instead of taxiing along a runway to build up enough speed to become airborne, as a conventional aeroplane has to do. As a result, much less space is required for take-off and landing.

Zeppelin
The name given by Count Ferdinand von Zeppelin to the airships built by his company. The first one flew in 1900, at Friedrichshafen on Lake Konstanz, and the last in 1939. They varied in length from 120 to 240 m, and their speeds ranged from 45 to 110 km/h.

Places to visit

The Science Museum, Exhibition Road, South Kensington, London;

Royal Air Force Museum, Grahame Park Way, Hendon, London;

Bristol City Museum, Queen's Road, Bristol (a full-size replica of the Bristol 'Boxkite');

British Balloon Museum and Library, in the Newbury District Museum, Newbury, Berks;

Cornwall Aero Park, Helston, Cornwall (a replica of Cody's 'Kite');

Imperial War Museum, Ducksford Airfield, Ducksford, Cambridgeshire;

Lincolnshire Aviation Museum, Old Railway Yard, Sleaford Road, Tattershall, Lincs; *postal address:* Lincolnshire Aviation Society, 24 Witham Bank West, Boston, Lincs.;

Museum of Flight, East Fortune Airfield, North Berwick, East Lothian;

Newark Air Museum, Newark Showground, Winthorpe Airfield, Newark, Notts.;

Norfolk and Suffolk Aviation Museum; *enquiries to:* J.C.Harne, Malthouse Cottage, Brooke, Norwich, Norfolk;

Open Air Museum, Beamish Hall, Stanley, Co. Durham;

Percy Pilcher Museum, Stanford Hall, Lutterworth, Leics.(a replica of the Pilcher 'Hawk');

Shuttleworth Collection, Old Warden Aerodrome, Biggleswade, Beds.

About the author

James Prunier (movable-wing monoplane)
Specifications:
Builder: Prunier-Laurensou (Normandy)
Launched: 25April 1959 at Oran, Algeria
Wingspan: 1.655 m (without feathers)
Length: 1.725 m
Unladen weight: 70 kg
Weight when fully loaded: 72 kg
Engine: 56–72 beats per minute (at rest)
Maximum speed: one double-page spread of this book per day
Fuel: likes red wine better than Indian ink
Special features: always in the clouds, but has never succeeded in taking off

James Prunier also wrote and illustrated **The Story of Trains**, in the *Discoverers* series. Ever since he was a child he had dreams of becoming a cartoonist. At art school he discovered his talent as an illustrator, and since then has never stopped working; his technique, his versatility and virtuosity have proved irresistible to publishers.

Other titles in the *Discoverers* series:

Discovering nature:
**Spring
Summer
Autumn
Winter
Flowers
The Book of the Sky
The Book of Rivers
The Book of the Forest
The Book of Deserts**

Discovering animals:
Your cat

Discovering history:
**Clothes through the Ages
Uniforms through the Ages
Ships and Seafarers
The Book of Inventions and Discoveries
Conquerors and Invaders
Sailors and Navigators**

Discovering transport:
The Story of Trains

Discovering Art:
Painting and Painters